BIG ENGLISH 4

T0345693

Contents

Kids in My Class

1 Read and look. Write the names.

Julia is serious. She likes reading. She has got blonde hair.

Tony has got short black hair. He's very friendly and funny.

Amelia has got straight hair. She is shy and plays the flute.

José is friendly and clever. He has got brown hair and wears glasses.

1 _____ **2** _____ **3** _____ **4** _____

2 Look at **1** and write **T** for true or **F** for false.

1 José wears glasses. _____

2 Amelia has got wavy hair. _____

3 Julia has got brown hair. _____

4 Tony is friendly. _____

5 Amelia is shy. _____

6 Tony is serious. _____

7 José has got black hair. _____

8 Julia likes reading. _____

3 Listen and write.

Who's That Girl?

It's the first day of school.
We're back in our classes.
Everybody looks different
And I've got new [1]_____!

Who's that girl
Standing over there?
She's taller [2]_____ me.
She's got [3]_____ dark hair.

In my class are the same friends I know.
But we all change. We all grow. (x2)

It's the first day of school
And I'm back in my chair.
Everybody looks different.
Now I've got [4]_____ hair.

Who's that girl?
Oh, wait, that's Marie!
Last time I saw her,
She was [5]_____ than me!

Chorus

4 Write sentences about two classmates.

Classmate 1: _____

_____

_____

Classmate 2: _____

_____

_____

5   Read. Then circle **Amanda** or **Christina**.

She's Just Like You!

There's a new girl in Christina's class at school. Her name is Amanda. She's got curly hair like Christina. But Christina's hair is shorter and curlier than Amanda's. Christina is taller than Amanda. They're both nice and they're both clever but Amanda is shy. Christina definitely isn't. Christina and Amanda are different in some ways but they've got a lot in common.

1   **Amanda / Christina** is a new student.

2   **Amanda / Christina** has got curlier hair.

3   **Amanda / Christina** has got longer hair.

4   **Amanda / Christina** is taller.

5   **Amanda / Christina** is shy.

6   Think about a classmate. Answer the questions.

1   What's his/her name?   _____

2   What colour is his/her hair?   _____

3   Is he/she tall or short?   _____

4   Is his/her hair long or short?   _____

THINK BIG   Think about a person in your family. Write about how you are the same and how you are different.   _____

1:09

7 **Listen and stick.**

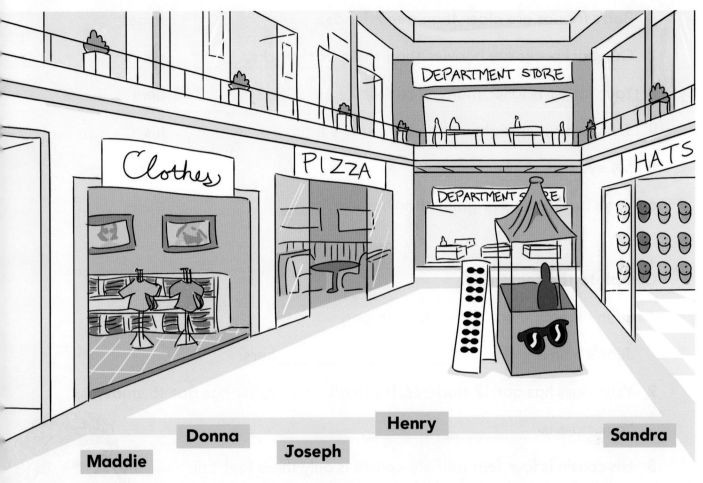

Donna

Maddie

Joseph

Henry

Sandra

8 **Complete the sentences.**

1 Maddie is _____ Henry. (*tall*)

2 Valerie's legs are _____ my legs. (*long*)

3 My mum's hair is _____ my hair. (*wavy*)

4 My school is _____ my brother's. (*big*)

5 This book is _____ that one. (*small*)

6 Jon's eyes are _____ his dad's eyes. (*light*)

9 **Look at 8 and complete new sentences.**

1 Henry is _____ Maddie.

2 My legs _____ Valerie's.

3 My hair is _____ my mum's.

4 My brother's school is _____ my school.

5 That book is _____ this one.

6 His dad's eyes are _____ Jon's.

Language in Action

10 **Read and match.**

1 Bob's friends are older than *our friends*.   mine

2 Our backpacks are heavier than *their backpacks*.   yours

3 Your father is taller than *my father*.   hers

4 José's hair is straighter than *his sister's hair*.   his

5 My eyes are darker than *your eyes*.   ours

6 Kim's backpack is brighter than *her dad's*.   theirs

11 **Complete the sentences.**

1 Juan's hair is short. *Kate's hair* is long.

Juan's hair is _____ hers.

2 Your class has got 12 students. It's small. *Their class* has got 15 students.

Your class is _____.

3 His cousin is four feet tall. *My cousin* is only three feet tall.

His cousin is _____.

4 *Our car* is big but your car is very big. Your car is

_____.

5 *Your hair* is black. His hair is brown. His hair is

_____.

6 *His book* is light. Her book is heavier. Her book is

_____.

7 *Their toys* are good. My toys are very good. My toys are

_____.

8 His singing is bad. *Her singing* is good. His singing is

_____.

12 Complete the sentences.

| common   fraternal   identical   rare   triplets |

1 A mother gives birth to Maria and Martin together. They don't look the same. They are _____ twins.

2 A mother gives birth to Tina, Gina and Nina together. They look the same. They are identical _____.

3 A mother gives birth to Bob and Rob together. They look the same. They are _____ twins.

4 Fraternal twins are more _____ than identical twins. Identical twins are very rare.

5 Quadruplets are very _____ – only about 1 out of every 9,000 births are quadruplets.

13 Read and choose the correct answers.

Identical quadruplets are very rare. But not if you're a nine-banded armadillo! It normally has FOUR identical babies at a time.

Some animals have more than one baby at a time but they aren't always identical. Cats usually give birth to 3–5 kittens and dogs usually have 5–10 puppies.

Some animals, such as elephants and some kinds of whales, almost never have more than one baby.

nine-banded armadillo

1 Nine-banded armadillos always have

a identical quadruplets.   **b** fraternal quadruplets.

2 Which animal never has triplets?

a an elephant   **b** a cat

3 Which animal almost always has only one baby at a time?

a a dog   **b** a whale

THINK BIG

Number in order from 1 (most common) to 5 (least common).

triplets ☐   identical twins ☐   quadruplets ☐

one baby ☐   fraternal twins ☐

14 **Read and circle T for true or F for false.**

A group of men in Germany started a competition in the 1990s. They compared their moustaches and beards. Soon, men from other countries like the United States, Norway and Switzerland also started competing. They held the World Beard and Moustache Championship every two years. Today the competition has got eighteen different categories.

1	The competition started in the United States.	**T**	**F**
2	In the competition, men compare beards and moustaches.	**T**	**F**
3	Men from Norway and Switzerland competed in the championship.	**T**	**F**
4	The championship is every two years.	**T**	**F**
5	There are eight different categories.	**T**	**F**

15 **Read and match.**

a

1 This man's beard looks like a star. He's competing in the Freestyle Beard category.

b

2 This man has got a long English Moustache. It's white and goes out on the sides.

c

3 This man is competing in The Verdi category. He's got a white beard and a curly moustache.

d

4 Look at this man's moustache! It's long and curls up. He looks like the famous painter Salvador Dalí.

16 **Read and number the parts of the paragraph.**

My Best Friend ← 1

My best friend's name is James. ← 2

He's shorter than me and his hair is darker than mine. James is shy and he is ← 3
funny, too. We like playing football at the weekend.

I'm happy to have a friend like James. ← 4

a detail sentences ☐   **b** final sentence ☐

c title ☐   **d** topic sentence ☐

17 **Read the paragraph. Circle the detail sentences. Copy the topic and final sentences.**

Mr Smith is my favourite teacher.
He's the music teacher at my school.
He can sing! He also plays the piano
and the guitar. He's also very clever
and he is funny, too. I'm happy to
have a teacher like Mr Smith.

Topic sentence: _____

_____

Final sentence: _____

_____

18 **Look at 17. Write about a favourite teacher.**

Topic sentence: _____

Detail 1: _____

Detail 2: _____

Detail 3: _____

Final sentence: _____

19 **Read and circle ear and air.**

year   fair   skirt

curly   pair   hear

chair   taller   more

hair   fear

20 **Underline the words with ear and air. Then read aloud.**

1 She's got small ears and curly fair hair.

2 I hear a pair of twins near the stairs.

21 **Connect the letters. Then write.**

| **1** y | | air | **a** _ _ _ _ _ |
| **2** ch | | ear | **b** _ _ _ _ |

1:17
22 **Listen and write.**

A boy with big ¹_____
And ²_____ hair,
Hears the twins on the
³
_____.
A boy with big ears and fair
⁴
_____,
⁵
_____ the twins sit on
Their chairs.

23 **Read and match.**

1 Twins are the
2 Identical twins look
3 Triplets are more
4 Quadruplets are

a very rare.
b common than quadruplets.
c most common.
d the same.

24 **Look and complete the sentences.**

glasses	serious
shorter	straight
taller	wavy

1 Mum's hair is _____.

2 Dad's hair is _____.

3 Mia is _____ than Tim.

4 Tim is _____ than Mia.

5 Grandma wears _____.

6 Mia likes to read. She is
_____.

25 **Rewrite the sentences.**

My hair is longer
than yours.

His hair is shorter
than mine.

1 My hair is longer than yours.
Your hair is shorter
_____.

2 Your brother is taller than mine.
My brother is shorter
_____.

3 His hair is curlier than hers.
Her hair is straighter
_____.

4 Her legs are shorter than his.
His legs are longer
_____.

5 Our car is brighter than theirs.
Their car is darker
_____.

6 Their house is smaller than ours.
Our house is bigger
_____.

Our Schedule

1 **Look and write.**

> eat   go (x3)   have   visit

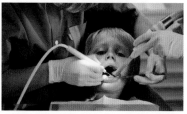

1 _____

2 _____

3 _____

4 _____

5 _____

6 _____

2 **Read and write the verbs.**

1 How often do you _____ to the dentist? I go twice a year.

2 I love going to restaurants so I _____ out once a month.

3 When we _____ on holiday, we love eating out.

4 My grandparents now live in Spain so we only _____ them in the summer and winter holidays.

5 Weddings are great fun but I don't _____ to them very often.

6 At my cousin's wedding I'm playing the guitar. I have to _____ lots of guitar lessons before the day!

3 **Listen and circle.**

Things We Do!

There are lots and lots of things
That I do every day,
Like go to school, **have / watch** a film,
Stay up late and play!

But there are lots of other things
I don't want to do so much,
Like **go / see** to the dentist, **make / do** the dishes,
Make / Do my bed and such.

How often do you do these things?
Every day? Once a week? Once a year?

I **take in / take out** the rubbish
On Tuesdays before school.
And I feed our funny cat,
But I don't mind — she's cool.

Chorus

4 **What about you? Complete the chart.**

once a day	I _____ _____ _____
twice a day	I _____ _____ _____
every night	I _____ _____ _____
every summer	I _____ _____ _____

Story

5 Read. Then circle.

A Lot of Weddings!

Christina and Amanda are talking about their plans for the weekend. Amanda is going to her grandma's house. She visits her grandma every week. Christina is going to her cousin's wedding. She goes to weddings three times a year. Christina doesn't like weddings because she has to wear a dress.

1 Amanda is going to her **cousin's** / **grandma's** house.

2 Amanda sees her grandma once a **week** / **month**.

3 Christina is going to her **brother's** / **cousin's** wedding.

4 Christina goes to three weddings a **year** / **week**.

6 Now answer the questions about you.

1 How often do you visit your grandma? _____

2 How often do you go to weddings? _____

3 What are you doing this weekend? _____

THINK
BIG **Think and write in order.**

every day   every Friday   once a year
three times a month   twice a day

not very often   ➤   ➤   ➤   ➤   ➤   very often

_____ _____ _____ _____ _____

_____ _____ _____ _____ _____

7 **Listen and stick. Number in order.**

a

b

c

d

8 **Circle the correct words.**

1 **What / Where** are they doing after school?

2 **What / Where** is she doing tomorrow?

3 **What / Where** are they going now?

4 **What / Where** is he doing after school?

5 **What / Where** are you doing on Saturday evening?

6 **What / Where** are we going on holiday?

9 **Look at the questions in 8. Match. Then write the answers. Use the words in the box.**

| eat out   go (x4)   visit |

a ☐ They _____ on holiday.

b ☐ He _____ his cousins.

c ☐ She _____ her uncle's wedding.

d ☐ We _____ to China.

e ☐ They _____ to the dentist.

f ☐ I _____ with my parents.

Language in Action

10 **Look at Laura's schedule. Answer the questions.**

This is my schedule.

| every day | once a week |
| twice a day | twice a week |

	Sun	Mon	Tue	Wed	Thu	Fri	Sat
play outside	✓	✓	✓	✓	✓	✓	✓
brush teeth	✓✓	✓✓	✓✓	✓✓	✓✓	✓✓	✓✓
take out the rubbish					✓		
have piano lessons		✓		✓			

1 How often does Laura play outside? _____

2 How often does Laura brush her teeth? _____

3 How often does Laura take out the rubbish? _____

4 How often does Laura have piano lessons? _____

11 **Read and match. Then complete.**

1 What are you doing this weekend?

a About _____ a week.

2 How often do you eat pizza?

b They're _____ to the zoo.

3 Where are they going this afternoon?

c I'm going _____ visit my friend.

12 **Match the sentences with the words.**

1 Lucy's got lots of friends.

2 Paul is good-looking.

3 This song goes with an advert.

4 Something I buy.

a a product

b a jingle

c attractive

d popular

13 **Look at the advert. Read and circle T for true or F for false.**

1 This advert uses a cartoon character to sell the product.   T   F

2 It uses a jingle to help you remember the product.   T   F

3 It tells you it will make you popular.   T   F

THINK BIG

Do you like the advert in 13? Why/Why not?
Use the words in the box.

colourful   design   famous   jingle   name   popular

I like/don't like _____

_____.

14 **Read and choose the correct answers.**

What unusual habits have you got?

🐦	**birdsong**	I live in Libya, Africa. It's REALLY hot all year. So I have a shower three times a day because it makes me feel clean and cool!
	racerXYZ	I've got a weird habit. I never touch doorknobs. I really like sliding doors because they haven't got doorknobs. It's lucky that I live in Tokyo, Japan.
❄	**snowflake**	My habits aren't really strange. Apart from one. I always drink COLD milk. I drink it twice a day but always WITH ICE. I love our milk in Hertfordshire, England. It's delicious.
	hatman22	I wear a hat every day to school. I even wear it in bed AND in the shower! It's cold here – in Rio Grande, Argentina.
📚	**ABCgirl**	You guys haven't got unusual habits. Listen to this! I always put the books on my shelf in alphabetical order and I HAVE TO check them every morning.

---

1 How often does birdsong have a shower?

  a once a day **b** twice a week
  c three times a day

2 Where is racerXYZ from?

  a Scotland **b** Japan **c** England

3 What does snowflake drink every day?

  a cola **b** milk **c** water

4 What does hatman22 wear in bed and in the shower?

  a hat **b** coat **c** gloves

5 What's the weather like in Rio Grande?

  a It's warm. **b** It's cool.
  c It's cold.

6 How often does ABC_girl look at her books?

  a every day **b** every week
  c once a month

15 **What do you do every day, week or month that is strange or unusual and why?**

---

16 **Read and circle the sequence words.**

> **My Day at School**
> First, we've got a Maths lesson. Next, we've got a spelling test. Then we have lunch. After that, we've got an English lesson. Finally, we've got a P.E. lesson.

17 **Read the paragraph. Look at 16. Write the sequence words.**

I am busy after school. ¹_____,
I have a snack. ²_____, I walk my
dog. ³_____ I play outside.
⁴_____, I eat dinner.
⁵_____, I do the dishes with my
brother and dad.

18 **What do you do after school? Add two more activities. Then number the six activities in order. Write a paragraph.**

☐ do homework   ☐ have a snack   ☐ _____
☐ eat dinner   ☐ play games   ☐ _____

_____

_____

_____

_____

_____

_____

19 **Read and circle ir and ur.**

bird   shirt   fur

dear   stairs   curl

ear   hurt   skirt

girl   surf

20 **Underline the words with ir and ur. Then read aloud.**

1 The girl is wearing a short skirt and a long T-shirt.

2 Pandas have got black and white fur.

21 **Connect the letters. Then write.**

1	s		urn	**a** _ _ _ _
2	t		urf	**b** _ _ _ _
3	b		urt	**c** _ _ _ _
4	h		ird	**d** _ _ _ _

1:34

22 **Listen and write.**

Two ¹_____ with red
²_____,
Two cats with black ³_____,
Two boys with white ⁴_____,
Are watching ⁵_____!

23 **Complete the dialogue.**

Ana: Hey, José! ¹_____ are you doing after school?

José: I'm really busy. ²_____, I'm visiting my grandmother.

Ana: Then what are you ³_____?

José: Then I'm meeting my mum.

Ana: ⁴_____ are you going?

José: We're ⁵_____ to the dentist.

Ana: Oh, no.

José: That's okay. ⁶_____, we ⁷_____ going to the cinema!

24 **Write the questions using How often. Then answer using the words in the box.**

do the dishes/twice a week   go on holiday/twice a year
play outside/every day   watch a DVD/once a week

1 _____?

He _____.

2 _____?

_____

3 _____?

_____

4 _____?

_____

Food Around the World

 Match. Write the letter.

1 _____ porridge	**a**	**b**	**2** _____ steamed buns
3 _____ paella	**c**	**d**	**4** _____ watermelon
5 _____ toasted cheese sandwich	**e**	**f**	**6** _____ cereal with milk
7 _____ lamb meatballs	**g**	**h**	**8** _____ noodle soup

2 **What food do you like?**

Breakfast: _____

Lunch: _____

Dinner: _____

3 **Listen and number in order. Which food is in the song? Tick (✓) or cross (✗).**

Would You Like Some?

"Come on, Sam. Just one little bite!"
"Oh, really, Dad. Oh, all right!
Mmm. Hey, you're right. It's great!
Please put some more on my plate!"

Come on, Sam, please have a little taste!
Come on, Sam, don't make a funny face!

"Would you like some chicken curry?"
"No thanks, Dad. I'm in a hurry!"
Sam says, "No, Dad, not right now
But thanks so much – thanks, anyhow."

"How about a sweet steamed bun?
It's really yummy. Come on, try one!"
Sam says, "No, Dad, not right now
But thanks so much – thanks, anyhow."

Chorus

"Would you like some noodle soup?
Tonight it tastes really nice!"
Sam says, "No, Dad, not right now.
But thanks so much – thanks, anyhow."

4 **Correct the strange food and write.**

1 steamed watermelon _____

2 porridge curry _____

3 toasted yoghurt sandwich _____

4 apple soup _____

5 cereal with lemonade _____

5 **Read. Then write T for true or F for false.**

Homemade Lemonade

Sam makes some cake and lemonade. He asks Christina to try them. Christina tries some cake but she doesn't like it. Then she tries the lemonade but it's horrible. It's too sour! Christina asks Sam what he put in the lemonade. He put in lemons, water and ice but he forgot the sugar!

1 Christina likes Sam's cake. _____

2 Christina thinks the lemonade tastes good. _____

3 The lemonade is sweet. _____

4 Sam put lemons in his lemonade. _____

5 Sam forgot to put sugar in his lemonade. _____

6 **Write about you. Answer Yes, I would or No, I wouldn't.**

1 Would you like to drink some lemon juice? _____

2 Would you like to eat some chocolate cake? _____

3 Would you like to drink some lemonade? _____

THINK BIG **What happens next in the story? Write.**

_____

_____

7 Listen and stick. Do they like the food? Tick (✓) or cross (✗).

1  ☐   **2**  ☐   **3** ☐    **4** ☐

8 Look and complete the questions and answers. Use **would like**.

Linda

Drinks

lemonade ☐
apple juice ☐
milk ✓

Lunch

lamb meatballs ☐
noodle soup ✓
steamed buns ☐

Paul

Drinks

lemonade ✓
apple juice ☐
milk ☐

Lunch

lamb meatballs ✓
noodle soup ☐
steamed buns ✓

Maria

Drinks

lemonade ☐
apple juice ✓
milk ☐

Lunch

lamb meatballs ☐
noodle soup ☐
steamed buns ☐

1 What _____ Linda _____?

_____

2 What _____ Paul _____?

_____

3 What _____ Maria _____?

_____

9 **Look at the pictures. Complete the sentences.**

1

A: _____ she _____ to have some pasta?

B: _____, she _____.

2

A: _____ he _____ to eat some porridge?

B: _____, he _____.

3

A: _____ they _____ to drink watermelon milkshakes?

B: _____, they _____.

4

A: _____ they _____ to try some curry?

B: _____, they _____.

10 **Complete for you.**

1 _____ you _____ to try _____?
Yes, I _____.

2 _____ you _____ to try _____?
No, I _____.

3 _____ your friend _____ to try _____?
Yes, he/she _____. No, he/she _____.

11 Circle the correct words.

1 For **a balanced** / **an unhealthy** diet, you should eat food from each of the five food groups every day.

2 The five food groups are: fruit, vegetables, dairy, protein and **chicken** / **grains**.

3 You should eat more **vegetables** / **dairy** than protein.

4 Don't eat food that is too **tasty** / **salty**.

5 Don't have drinks with a lot of **sugar** / **water** in them.

12 Write the food on the plate.

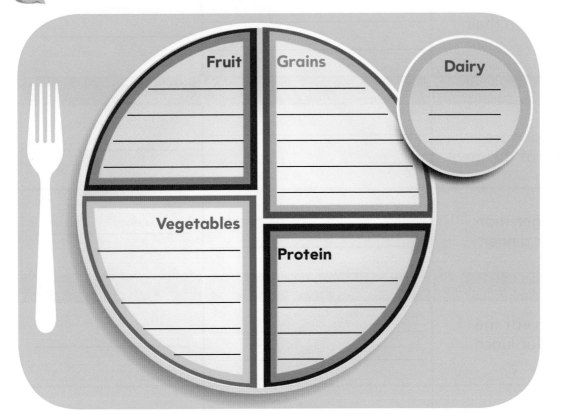

bananas
beans
bread
carrots
cereal
cheese
chicken
fish
mangoes
milk
oranges
pasta
peppers
potatoes
rice
yoghurt

Who has the most balanced diet? Complete the sentences.

THINK BIG

John has cereal with milk, a mango, a chicken sandwich, a salad and a yoghurt.

Jenny has a cheese and pepperoni pizza, a yoghurt, a glass of milk and some crisps.

¹_____ has a balanced diet. ²_____ doesn't have a balanced diet. He/She eats too much ³_____ and ⁴_____ and not enough ⁵_____, ⁶_____ or ⁷_____.

13 **Read 18 on page 36 of your Pupil's Book.**
Then write about *your* school lunches.
What is the same/different?

What do they eat for lunch in Brazil?

Japan	_____ (my country)	Same or Different?
Kids take turns serving.		
Kids eat lunch in their classroom.		
Brazil		
Rice and beans are always part of the meal.		
Lunch is bigger than breakfast or dinner.		
Zambia		
People often eat the same thing for lunch and dinner.		
People eat some food with their hands.		
Italy		
Food is often organic or grown naturally.		
Kids eat meat for lunch once or twice a week.		

14 **Read and write so or because.**

> **1** I love eating paella _____ I have it twice a week.
>
> **2** I don't like eating chicken curry _____ I don't like spicy food.

15 **Match and circle the conjunctions.**

1 She doesn't like milk

2 It's cold today

3 I often have a toasted cheese sandwich for breakfast

4 We love eating meatballs

5 Carlos likes paella

6 I eat a balanced diet

a so we eat them every week.

b because I want to be healthy.

c so I'm having porridge for breakfast.

d because he's Spanish.

e so she doesn't drink it.

f because I like cheese a lot.

16 **Join the sentences and write. Use so and because.**

1 I'm wearing a coat. It's cold.

_____

2 I don't like fruit. I don't eat watermelon.

_____

3 Sally is happy. She's eating her favourite lunch.

_____

17 **Read and circle le, el, al and il.**

apple curl pupil

pencil medal sandal

hear

camel hair

bubble travel

18 **Underline the words with le, el, al and il. Then read aloud.**

1 There are apples in April.

2 I wear sandals when I travel in summer.

19 **Connect the letters. Then write.**

1 app   el   **a** _ _ _ _ _

2 pup   le   **b** _ _ _ _ _

3 cam   al   **c** _ _ _ _ _

4 med   il   **d** _ _ _ _ _

20 **Listen and write.**

Take your ¹ _____,

Draw a ² _____,

Draw a ³ _____,

Draw some ⁴ _____.

21 **Write questions or answers.**

1 What would she like for breakfast?

_____

2 _____

He'd like a toasted cheese sandwich for lunch.

3 What would they like for dinner?

_____

4 _____

They'd like chicken curry for dinner.

5 What would you like for dinner?

_____

22 **Complete the dialogue. Write would or wouldn't.**

Mum: ¹_____ you like to go to the Indian restaurant?

Bobby: No, I ²_____ .

Mum: ³_____ you like to go to the Italian restaurant?

Bobby: No, I ⁴_____ .

Mum: Where ⁵_____ you like to go for dinner?

Bobby: I ⁶_____ like to go to a sweet shop!

23 **Read and match.**

1 Eat more grains   **a** balanced diet.

2 Don't eat too   **b** much salt.

3 Have a lot of   **c** than protein.

4 Have a   **d** fruit.

My Robot

1 **Choose and draw one path. Design a robot.**

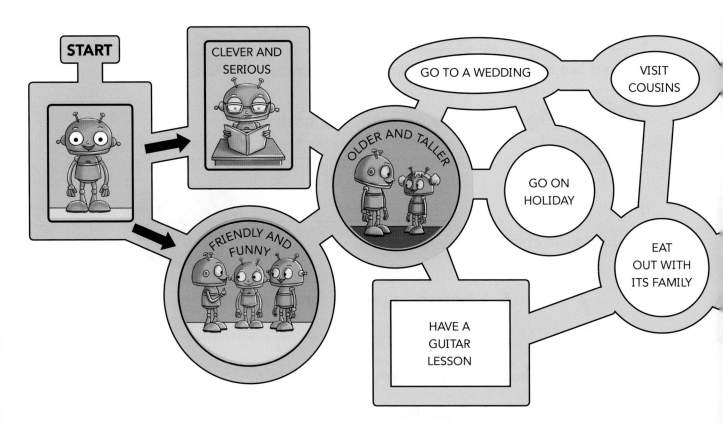

2 **Look at your path in 1. Answer the questions with words from your path.**

What is the robot like? _____

What is it doing today? _____

What would it like to try? _____

3 **Look at your path in 1 and ✓ the word or words.**

My robot likes ☐ spicy ☐ salty ☐ sweet ☐ sour food.

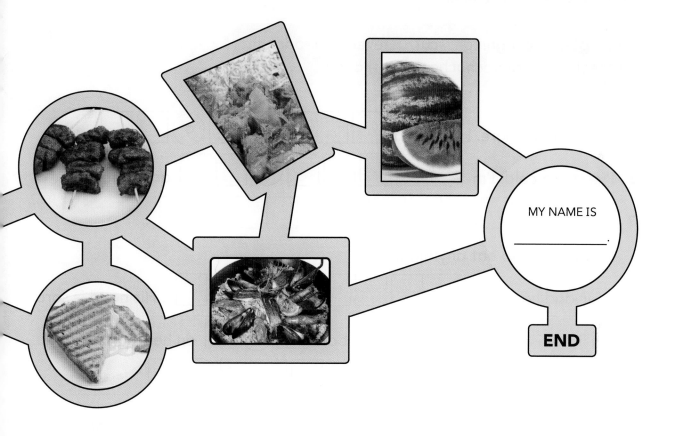

MY NAME IS

_____.

END

4 **Look at the information about your robot. Give it a name.
Write a paragraph about it.**

_____

_____

_____

_____

_____

_____

unit 4 How Do You Feel?

1 **Complete the sentences.**

> allergies   coughing   cut   fever   headache
> sneezing   stomachache   toothache

1 His teeth are sore. He's got a ⬜⬜⬜⬜⬜ⓐ⬜⬜⬜ .

2 I've got a cold. I'm ⬜⬜⬜⬜⬜◯⬜⬜ and I feel tired.

3 I've got ◯⬜⬜⬜⬜⬜⬜⬜⬜⬜⬜ .

I don't want to eat anything.

4 Your dad has got a ⬜⬜⬜⬜⬜◯⬜⬜ . His head is sore.

5 My little sister fell. Now she's got a bad ⬜ⓤ⬜ on her leg.

6 Your head feels hot. You must have a ⬜⬜⬜◯⬜ .

7 My mum has got bad ⬜◯⬜⬜⬜⬜⬜⬜ . She's ⬜⬜◯⬜⬜⬜◯⬜ a lot.

2 **Write the letters from the circles in 1. Use the letters to complete the joke.**

ⓐ ◯ ◯ ◯ ⓤ ◯ ◯ ◯ ◯

Doctor, my son ate my pen! What should I do?

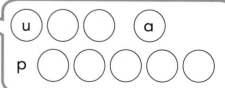

ⓤ ◯ ◯ ⓐ
p ◯ ◯ ◯ ◯ ◯

3 **Listen and write. Use the words in the box.**

Stay in Bed and Rest!

You're ¹_____
And you're ²_____ .
You need to stay in bed.
I think you've got a fever.
Here, let me feel your head.
You shouldn't go to school today.
You should ³_____ instead.

When you're ill or feeling blue,
Your family takes good care of you.

You've got a ⁴_____
And a ⁵_____ .
Here's what I suggest:
You should drink some ⁶_____
And juice.
⁷_____ and rest!
Listen to your dad, now,
Taking care of yourself is best.

Chorus

cold   coughing   fever
sneezing   stay home
Stay in bed   tea

4 **Read and choose the correct answers.**

When you're ill, here's what I suggest:

1 You shouldn't
  a stay in bed.   **b** go to school.   **c** stay home.

2 You shouldn't
  a run around.   **b** rest.   **c** drink water.

3 You shouldn't
  a go to a doctor.   **b** eat sweets.   **c** take care of yourself.

5 **Read. Then answer the questions.**

You're Hurt!

Sam and Christina are having lunch together. Sam sees something red on Christina's arm. He gets upset because he thinks Christina has got a cut. He tells Christina that she should go to see the nurse and put a plaster on her arm. But Christina tells him that it's not blood on her arm – it's ketchup! She's alright but she needs a napkin.

1 What are Sam and Christina doing? _____

2 Who does Sam think Christina should see? _____

3 What does Sam think Christina should do? _____

6 **Read. Then complete the sentences.**

nurse   plaster   rest   run

I fell over and cut my knee. Ouch!

You should _____

_____.

_____.

You shouldn't _____.

THINK BIG **Look at 5 again. What happens next in the story? Write.**

_____

_____

7 **Listen and stick. Number in order and write.**

2:08

a

He should go to the _____.

b

She should go to the _____.

c

She should take some _____.

d

He should eat some soup and get some _____.

8 **Read and circle.**

1 I **should / shouldn't** eat vegetables.

2 He **should / shouldn't** exercise every day.

3 We **should / shouldn't** stay up late.

4 They **should / shouldn't** eat healthy food.

9 **Read and write should or shouldn't.**

1 **Joe:** I've got a headache.

  Doctor: You _____ drink some water.

2 **Dad:** My children have got allergies.

  Doctor: They _____ stay inside and take medicine.

3 **Mum:** My son has got a fever.

  Doctor: He _____ go to school.

4 **Sonya:** I like watching TV for hours every day.

  Doctor: You _____ watch so much TV.

10 **Read and ✓.**

1 I go to bed late and eat a lot of crisps. I should take better care of _____.

   a ☐ myself   **b** ☐ yourself   **c** ☐ herself

2 You never eat fruit. You should take better care of _____.

   a ☐ myself   **b** ☐ yourself   **c** ☐ ourselves

3 She does a lot of exercise. She takes good care of _____.

   a ☐ himself   **b** ☐ themselves **c** ☐ herself

4 We eat a healthy breakfast. We take good care of _____.

   a ☐ myself   **b** ☐ ourselves   **c** ☐ themselves

5 They watch TV all the time. They should take better care of _____.

   a ☐ themselves **b** ☐ ourselves   **c** ☐ herself

6 He always washes his hands. He takes good care of _____.

   a ☐ herself   **b** ☐ myself   **c** ☐ himself

11 **Read the problems. Write advice.**

1 I'm coughing and I've got a sore throat.

_____

2 My brother has got a cut on his leg.

_____

3 My friends don't eat vegetables.

_____

4 I've got stomachache.

_____

5 I stay up late every night.

_____

12 **Read and write.**

| clean | fungi | microscope | toothbrush | toxin | viruses |

About Germs

very small – we need a ¹_____ to see them

make a poison called a ²_____

cause illness

Where are Germs?

sink and bath

³_____

TV remote control

computer keyboard

Germs

Kinds of Germs

bacteria

protozoa

⁴_____

⁵_____

How to Protect Yourself

wash hands

keep the house

⁶_____

13 **Read and answer.**

1 How many kinds of germs are there? _____

2 Can germs make us ill? _____

3 Where can germs get into the home? _____

4 How can we stay away from germs? _____

THINK BIG

Think and ✓ or ✗. Can you find germs on a...?

library book ☐   computer mouse ☐   toilet ☐   coin ☐

phone ☐   door ☐   toy ☐   water fountain ☐

Which place do you think has the most germs? Why?

14 **Read and write.**

Cinnamon   Garlic   Ginger

¹_____ is used around the world as a home remedy for many different problems. For example, many people take ginger when they've got stomachache. In Japan, mothers give their children tea made from ginger and sugar when they've got a cold. In Europe, people drink hot water with ginger, honey and lemon to help with sore throats.

²_____ is also a common home remedy. In Spain, people add garlic to their tea to help with colds and coughs. Some Native Americans put garlic on a bee sting. The garlic helps stop the sting from hurting.

³_____ is another common home remedy. Many people use it for colds but did you know you can also use it to help with toothaches? Just mix some cinnamon with honey and put it on the sore tooth. This not only helps the tooth from hurting but tastes delicious, too.

15 **Look at 14 and ✓.**

	bee sting	cold	sore throat	stomachache	toothache
ginger					
garlic					
cinnamon					

16 **What else do people use cinnamon, garlic and ginger for?**

cinnamon: _____

garlic: _____

ginger: _____

17 **Are commas used correctly? Read and ✓ or ✗.**

> **1** **a** First, I eat a healthy breakfast. Then I go swimming.
>
>   **b** First I eat a healthy breakfast. Then, I go swimming.
>
> **2** **a** You should drink some tea take some medicine and sleep.
>
>   **b** You should drink some tea, take some medicine and sleep.
>
> **3** **a** I take good care of myself. She takes good care of herself too.
>
>   **b** I take good care of myself. She takes good care of herself, too.

18 **Add commas in the correct places.**

1 I get a lot of rest drink water exercise and eat fruit.

2 I don't eat cookies cake chocolate or sweets.

3 First I should eat a healthy dinner. Then I should do my homework. Finally I should go to bed.

4 The four kinds of germs are bacteria fungi protozoa and viruses.

5 You should drink some tea. You should take some medicine too.

6 First he should take some medicine. After that he should have some soup.

19 **Write answers. Remember to use commas.**

1 I want to eat a healthy lunch. What should I eat?

_____

_____

2 I want to be healthy and exercise. What should I do?

_____

_____

3 I've got stomachache and a fever. What should I do?

_____

_____

20 **Read and circle kn and wr.**

knee   breakfast   wrist

knight   write   wrong

know

knock

now   wrap   right

21 **Underline the words with kn and wr. Then read aloud.**

1 The knight knows how to write.

2 He wraps his knee and knots the rope.

22 **Connect the letters. Then write.**

1 kn   eck   **a** _ _ _ _ _

2 wr   ock   **b** _ _ _ _ _

2:17

23 **Listen and write.**

What's wrong, ¹_____, wrong?

The ²_____ knocked his
Knee, knee, knee
And his wrist, wrist, ³_____.

I ⁴_____! Wrap his knee

And ⁵_____ his wrist!

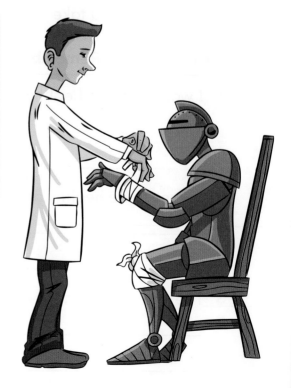

Read and match.

1 We have to
2 Germs make
3 Bacteria is
4 Germs get into

a one kind of germ.
b many places.
c protect ourselves from germs.
d a kind of poison called a toxin.

 Read and circle.

1 She stays up late every night. She should take better care of **himself** / **herself**.
2 They take good care of **themselves** / **ourselves**. They exercise every morning.
3 I eat a lot of crisps. I should take better care of **myself** / **yourself**.
4 You always eat a healthy lunch. You take good care of **yourself** / **ourselves**.

26 **Look and write. Then complete the sentences with should or shouldn't.**

| allergies | cut | fever | headache | sore throat | stomachache |

1 She's got a _____. She _____ drink water and rest.

2 He's got a _____. He _____ talk too much.

3 She's got a _____. She _____ go to school.

4 He's got _____. He _____ eat so many sweets.

5 She's got _____. She _____ go outside.

6 He's got a _____. He _____ take better care of himself.

unit 5 Weird and Wild Animals

1 **Look and write. Then match.**

> angler fish   coconut crabs   tarsiers   Tasmanian devils   volcano rabbits

1 _____

a They've got long teeth and they live in oceans all over the world. We don't know how many there are.

2 _____

b They've got big eyes and brown fur. They live in Southeast Asia but we don't know their population.

3 _____

c They've got a population of more than 100,000 and they live on islands in the Pacific Ocean. They're orange and brown.

4 _____

d They've got grey fur and they live on volcanoes in Mexico. They've got a population of between 2,000 and 12,000.

5 _____

e They've got black and white fur. They've got a population of between 10,000 and 25,000 and you can find them in Tasmania.

2 Listen and write. Then draw.

♪ Understanding Animals

Do you know a lot about animals?
How many different kinds there are?
Some are ¹_____ and
Some are ²_____
And some are just bizarre!

Understanding animals is good for us to do
Because learning about animals helps us
And helps them, too!

Some live in ³_____ or in the
⁴_____
And some live where it's hot.
Some are beautiful and some are cute
And some are... well, they're not!

Chorus

It's important to learn about animals,
Though many seem strange, it's true.
Because when we learn about animals,
We learn about ourselves, too.

Chorus

3 Write the animals.

big	small	live in trees	live in the sea

4 **Read. Then complete the sentences.**

Chimps are Clever!

Christina is watching a TV programme about chimpanzees. She learns that chimps are clever and amazing animals. They can climb trees, talk to other chimps and use tools to get food. But there are not many chimps left in the wild. They are endangered because people are moving into their habitat. Sam can talk, climb trees and use tools to get food, too. He hopes he isn't endangered!

1 Christina is watching a programme about _____, or chimps.

2 Chimps are _____ and amazing animals.

3 They can climb trees and _____ to each other.

4 Chimps use _____ to get food.

5 There aren't many chimps in the wild – they are _____.

5 **Answer about you.**

1 Can you do any of the things that chimps can do?

_____

2 Do you like chimps? Why/Why not?

_____

THINK BIG **Chimps use tools to get food. What tools do you use to...**

a cook/eat food? _____

b do your homework? _____

c stay clean? _____

2:25

6 **Listen and stick. Then write.**

1

2

3

1990s: more than 100,000

100 years ago: about 100,000

100 years ago: about 90,000

Now: _____

Now: _____

Now: _____

7 **Read and complete.**

		There were...	There are...
	Komodo dragon	How many? *more than 20,000* When? *fifty years ago*	How many? *fewer than 5,000* When? *now*
	Andean condor	How many? *many* When? *in the past*	How many? *about 10,000* When? *now*
	Tasmanian devil	How many? *100,000* When? *twenty-five years ago*	How many? *between 10,000 and 25,000* When? *now*

1 A: _____ [_____] _____ in the past?

B: _____ many. Now _____ about 10,000.

2 A: _____ [_____] _____ twenty-five years ago?

B: _____ 100,000. Now _____ between 10,000 and 25,000.

3 A: _____ [_____] _____ fifty years ago?

B: _____ more than 20,000. Now _____ fewer than 5,000.

Language in Action

8 Why are they endangered? Follow each maze and complete the dialogues.

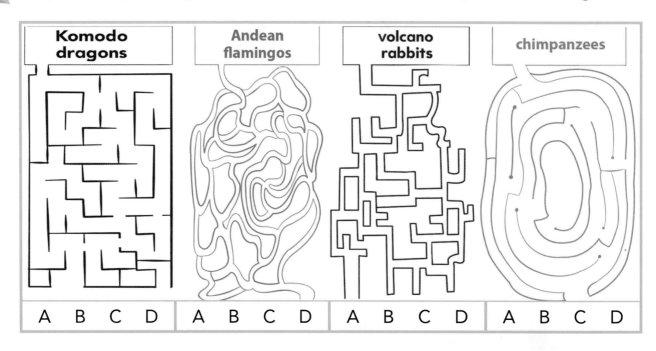

Komodo dragons	Andean flamingos	volcano rabbits	chimpanzees
A B C D	A B C D	A B C D	A B C D

A = Their habitat's polluted.   C = People are moving into their habitat.

B = People are killing them.   D = People are destroying their habitat.

1 A: _____ are Komodo dragons endangered?

B: They're endangered _____ [   ].

2 A: _____ are Andean flamingos endangered?

B: They're endangered _____ [   ].

3 A: _____ are volcano rabbits endangered?

B: They're endangered _____ [   ].

4 A: _____ are chimpanzees endangered?

B: They're endangered _____ [   ].

9 Write the question and answer.

_____

_____ (coconut crabs)?

_____

_____ (people destroying their habitat).

10 **Complete the sentences.**

> bamboo   bumblebee   extinct   polluted   scientists   wild

1 _____ bats are endangered because farmers burn trees where they live. There aren't many left in the _____.

2 Most red pandas live in China and the Himalayas and they eat _____ leaves. They're endangered because people are destroying the bamboo forests.

3 Egyptian tortoises are very small – they're only 10 centimetres long. Many _____ believe there are only 7,500 left in the wild now because people keep them as pets.

4 Mexican walking fish are almost _____.They lived in streams and ponds but their habitats are now _____.

11 **Why is each animal endangered? Look at 10. Then write the names and match.**

1    **2**    **3**    **4**

_____   _____   _____   _____

_____   _____   _____   _____

a   **b**   **c**   **d**

Which animals are extinct? Circle.

THINK BIG

1 tiger / chimpanzee / giant panda / dodo

2 Asian elephant / mountain gorilla / T-rex / blue whale

3 orangutan / bumblebee bat / woolly mammoth / red panda

2:29

12 **Listen, read and circle.**

1 In North America and Europe, dragons are
- **good** / **evil**
- **fire-breathing** / **real**
- **funny** / **scary**

2 In China, Japan and Korea, dragons are
- beautiful and **magical** / **evil**
- **fire-breathing** / **helpful**
- **scary** / **not scary**

3 In Oceania and Australia, one dragon is
- called a **Western** / **Bunyip**
- **friendly** / **scary**
- made of different parts of different **animals** / **people**

4 In Indonesia, dragons are
- **real** / **mythical**
- **large lizards** / **birds**
- **extinct** / **endangered**

13 **Look at 12. Read and circle T for true or F for false.**

1 In North America and Europe, dragons are evil.   T   F
2 Dragons in China are made up of different animal parts.   T   F
3 In Oceania, dragons are scary.   T   F
4 Dragons are extinct in Indonesia.   T   F
5 In Japan, dragons are fire-breathing.   T   F
6 In Indonesia, dragons are large lizards.   T   F

14 **Look and match.**

1 exclamation mark
2 full stop
3 question mark

15 **Write a full stop, a question mark or an exclamation mark.**

1 How many chimps were there 100 years ago____

2 Coconut crabs live on islands in the Pacific Ocean____

3 Wow____ That frog is so amazing____

4 Why are chimps endangered____

5 Look____ A dragon____

6 They've got a population of 100,000____

16 **Write sentences. Use a full stop, a question mark or an exclamation mark.**

1

angler fish

_____

_____

2

tigers

_____

_____

3

Tasmanian devils

_____

_____

4

volcano rabbits

_____

_____

5

Andean condors

_____

_____

6

black rhinos

_____

_____

17 **Read and circle ph and wh.**

phone **panda** **wheel**

phantom **white** **wild**

photo

whale

dolphin **fish** **wheat**

18 **Underline the words with ph and wh. Then read aloud.**

1 When was the white elephant in the wheat?

2 I took a photo with my phone of a whale and a dolphin.

19 **Connect the letters. Then write.**

1 ph   en   **a** _ _ _ _

2 wh   one   **b** _ _ _ _ _

2:34

20 **Listen and write.**

The phantom's got a ¹_____
On his ²_____
Of a ³_____ wheel
And some ⁴_____.

21 **Unscramble and complete.**

1 Some scientists believe there are fewer than 7,500 Egyptian tortoises left in the _____. (*ldiw*)

2 Most bumblebee bats live in _____ in Thailand. (*vesac*)

3 Red pandas eat _____ leaves. (*ooambb*)

4 Most scientists believe that the Mexican walking fish is almost _____. (*cnetxit*)

22 **Complete the dialogues with words from the box.**

because	chimpanzees	coconut crabs
habitat	How many	tarsiers
There are	There were	Why

1

A: Why are _____ endangered?

B: They're endangered _____ people are destroying their _____.

2

A: _____ Andean condors are there now?

B: _____ only about 10,000 left in the wild.

3

A: How many _____ were there a hundred years ago?

B: _____ over a million.

4

A: _____ are _____ endangered?

B: They're endangered because people are eating them.

Life Long Ago

1 **Read and write the letters. Then trace the path.**

L travel by car
I travelled by horse and carriage
G had oil lamps
E listened to the radio
N cook in a microwave
O washed clothes by hand

L wash clothes in a washing machine
G cooked on a coal stove
A have electric lights
F listen to an mp3 player
O have a mobile phone
! used a phone with an operator

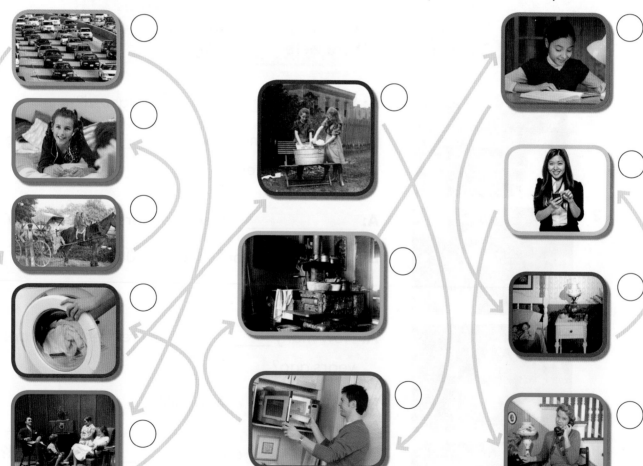

2 **Look at the letters in 1. Follow the path and write the letters. What do they spell?**

___ ___ ___ ___ ___ ___ ___ ___ ___ ___ ___ ___ ___ ___

3 **Listen and match.**

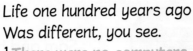

In the Old Days

a

Now there's water
from the tap.

Life one hundred years ago
Was different, you see.
¹ There were no computers
² And there was no TV.

Life was different in the old days.
Life was different in so many ways.

³ Children used to get water
From pumps or wells outdoors.
Now we just turn on the tap
And out fresh water pours!

Chorus

Life was so much slower!
⁴ Few people had a car.
⁵ Children used to walk to school
And they walked very far!

Chorus

b

Now there's TV.

c

Now there
are computers.

d

Now kids take
a school bus.

e

Now lots of people have got cars.

4 **Write about now and long ago.**

Now

Long Ago

_____ _____

_____ _____

_____ _____

_____ _____

_____ _____

_____ _____

5 **Read. Then circle T for true or F for false.**

Life was Nicer Then

Sam and his grandma are watching the TV. Sam wants to change the channel but he's too lazy to get the TV remote control. They didn't have remote controls when Sam's grandma was a child. They used to walk to the TV to change the channel. They only had three channels when Grandma was young and she thinks life was nicer then.

The microwave beeps. Grandma sometimes uses a microwave to make dinner. Maybe some things about modern life are nicer!

1 Grandma is too lazy to change the channel.   T   F

2 People didn't watch TV when Sam's grandma was young.   T   F

3 There were no remote controls when Sam's grandma was a child.   T   F

4 There are only three channels now.   T   F

5 Grandma uses a microwave to cook.   T   F

What did your grandma have when she was a child? Read and ✓ or ✗. Then write.

THINK BIG

computer ☐   phone ☐   washing machine ☐   microwave ☐
car ☐   bike ☐   TV remote control ☐   books ☐   radio ☐

My grandma had _____

_____.

She didn't have _____

_____.

2:42

6 **Listen and stick. Number in order.**

a
 ☐

b
 ☐

c
 ☐

d
 ☐

7 **Read and write the answers. Use did or didn't.**

1 **A:** Did your grandmother have a TV when she was young?

B: _____

2 **A:** Did people have cars fifty years ago?

B: _____

3 **A:** Did your grandfather play video games when he was a child?

B: _____

4 **A:** Did people have washing machines 200 hundred years ago?

B: _____

8 **Complete the questions and answers.**

1

A: _____ mum _____ a mobile phone at school?

B: _____, _____. She used public phones.

2

A: _____ dad _____ a computer at school?

B: _____, _____. It was big and slow.

9 **Complete the sentences.**

1 **A:** Before computers, how _____

keep in touch?

B: They _____.

2 **A:** Before washing machines, how _____

wash clothes?

B: They _____.

3 **A:** Before electricity, what _____

for light?

B: They _____.

4 **A:** Before cars, what _____

for transportation?

B: They _____.

10 **Answer about you.**

1 When she was young, what did your grandma use to do at night?

_____

2 When you were six, how did you use to go to school?

_____

11 **Look in your house. What used to be different?**

1 _____

_____

2 _____

_____

3 _____

_____

12 **Read and solve the equations.**

Horse and Carriage	Model T	Modern Car

A horse and carriage had an average speed of 8 kilometres (km) per hour.	A Model T had an average speed of 40 kilometres (km) per hour.	A modern car has an average speed of 90 kilometres (km) per hour.

1 A horse and carriage travels for 10 hours. How far does it travel?

_____ X _____ = _____ km

average speed   number of hours   distance travelled

2 A Model T travels for 6 hours. How far does it travel?

_____ X _____ = _____ km

3 A horse and carriage travels for 8 hours. How far does it travel?

_____ X _____ = _____ km

4 A modern car travels for 2 hours. How far does it travel?

_____ X _____ = _____ km

5 A Model T travels for 7 hours. How far does it travel?

_____ X _____ = _____ km

6 A modern car travels for 3 hours. How far does it travel?

_____ X _____ = _____ km

THINK BIG

Look at 12 and cross out the answers. Then use the other numbers to make a new equation.

| 3 | 40 | 64 | 80 | 120 | 180 | 240 | 270 | 280 |

A Model T travels for _____ hours. How far does it travel?

_____ X _____ = _____ km

13 **Read and write.**

> ancestors   forests   language   nomadic   reindeer   tundra

The Hmong

The Hmong people live in Southeast Asia and they've got their own way of life and their own ¹_____. You won't find much modern technology in a traditional Hmong village because people there live the way their ²_____ did 2,000 years ago.

The Maasai

The Maasai of Kenya are ³_____. This means they move from place to place and make new homes each time. They often live in ⁴_____ and build their homes out of things they can find in nature.

The Koryak

The Koryak live in the northern part of Russia's Pacific coast. Their land is Arctic ⁵_____ and it is very cold. For food, they herd ⁶_____ and catch fish. Koryak children wear warm hats made of reindeer skins.

14 **Look at 13 and ✓.**

	The Hmong	The Koryak	The Maasai
1 live in Russia			
2 move from place to place			
3 live in Southeast Asia			
4 wear reindeer skin hats			
5 live in Kenya			
6 live like people did 2,000 years ago			

15 **Put speech marks in the correct places.**

1 Did they watch films in the 1920s? he asked.

2 I used to play football, said John.

3 Jamie yelled, I got a new bike!

4 Karen said, I wrote a letter last night.

16 **Rewrite the sentences. Use said or asked and speech marks.**

How did people travel in 1905?

Did you use to ride in a horse and carriage?

They used to ride in a horse and carriage.

I'm not that old!

Ed   Mum

1 _____

2 _____

3 _____

4 _____

17 **Look and write what they are saying. Use said, asked or yelled and speech marks.**

_____	_____

1  **2**

18 **Read and circle ge and dge.**

fridge   cage   watched

traditional   washed   large

badge

edge   page   age

bridge

19 **Underline the words with ge and dge. Then read aloud.**

1 Look over the edge of the hedge. There's a bridge.

2 The boy's wearing a large badge and carrying a cage.

20 **Connect the letters. Then write.**

1 ca   dge   **a** _ _ _ _

2 ba   ge   **b** _ _ _ _ _

3 lar   ge   **c** _ _ _ _

4 e   dge   **d** _ _ _ _ _

2:50
21 **Listen and write.**

There's a ¹ _____ fridge

On the ² _____ .

There's a large ³ _____

In the ⁴ _____ .

22 **Read and solve the equations.**

1 A school bus has an average speed of 60 kilometres per hour. How far does it travel in 3 hours?

_____ X _____ = _____ km

2 A bike has an average speed of 20 kilometres per hour. How far does it travel in 6 hours?

_____ X _____ = _____ km

23 **Circle and write.**

1 **A: Did / Do** people have microwaves 100 years ago?

B: _____

2 **A:** Did your city or town **had / have** cars ten years ago?

B: _____

3 **A:** Did people **use to / used to** listen to mp3 players before electricity?

B: _____

4 **A:** Did your dad **travel / travelled** to school by horse and carriage?

B: _____

24 **Circle four things that didn't exist long ago. Write sentences with didn't use to.**

1 _____

2 _____

3 _____

4 _____

Sue's Path

1 Look at Units 4, 5 and 6. Choose words from the units. Write them in the charts.

2 Draw one path. Gather information and add your own.

HEALTH PROBLEMS

_____ _____

_____ _____

_____ _____

_____

Sue

START

Headache

Doctor

Medicine

Toothache

Your Own Information

Rest

Watch TV

Dentist

Why is Sue sad? What should she do?

END

3 Look at 1 and 2. Gather information and answer the questions. Write a paragraph and explain your answer.

_____

_____

_____

_____

ENDANGERED ANIMALS

_____

_____

_____

_____

TECHNOLOGY NOW

_____

_____

_____

_____

END

Endangered Animals

TIGERS:
Used to be
100,000.
Fewer than
3,200!

KOMODO
DRAGON:
Used to be
20,000.
Fewer than
5,000!

Why
are they
endangered?
What should
we do?

END

Long Ago
and Now

Your Own
Information

What did
people use?
What do they
use now?

Special Days

1 **Look and write the special days.**

1 _____

2 _____

3 _____

4 _____

5 _____

6 _____

2 **Read and circle T for true or F for false.**

1 My parents' anniversary is celebrated by my mum and dad.   **T**   **F**

2 New Year's Day is before New Year's Eve.   **T**   **F**

3 School Sports Day is for parents, not kids.   **T**   **F**

4 My dad celebrates Father's Day.   **T**   **F**

3 **Listen and write. Use the words in the box.**

What Do We Do on Special Days?

This ¹_____ is a special day –
The last day of the year.
We're ²_____ stay up very late.
At midnight we're going to cheer!

Special days are cool. Special days are fun.
Special days bring special treats for everyone!

On the first of ³_____,
We are going to say,
"Happy New Year!" to everyone
Because it's ⁴_____.

Chorus

There are lots of special days
And this one is a treat.
We're going to
Have ⁵_____
And ⁶_____
And delicious food to eat!

Chorus

fireworks
Friday
going to
January
New Year's Day
parades

4 **Look at 3 and ✓.**

1 This Friday is

☐ 30ᵗʰ December.   ☐ 31ˢᵗ December.   ☐ 1ˢᵗ January.

2 They are going to cheer

☐ at lunchtime.   ☐ in the afternoon.   ☐ at midnight.

3 On New Year's Eve they

☐ stay up late.   ☐ go to bed early.   ☐ sleep late.

Story

5 **Read. Then answer the questions.**

The Anniversary Party

Sam knows his parents' wedding anniversary is the 10th. He's planning a big celebration for their anniversary on 10th June. They're going to go out for a special dinner. Sam is making a cake. His parents like the plans but there's a problem. Their anniversary is on 10th July, not 10th June!

1 Why is Sam planning a celebration? _____

2 Where are they going to go? _____

3 What's the problem? _____

6 **Write about you and your family.**

1 My birthday is on _____.

2 My mum's birthday is on _____.

3 My dad's birthday is on _____.

4 My parents' wedding anniversary is on _____.

THINK BIG

Think and write. What do you think Sam's parents are going to say next?

_____

_____

3:09

7 Listen and stick. Then listen and write the special day and what they are going to do.

1

_____

_____

2

_____

_____

3

_____

_____

8 Answer the questions about Sarah's calendar.

Sun	Mon	Tue	Wed	Thu	Fri	Sat
1	**2**	**3** Today	**4**	**5**	**6**	**7** Birthday party
8	**9**	**10**	**11** Parents' anniversary	**12**	**13**	**14** Sister visits friend
15	**16**	**17**	**18** Watch parade	**19**	**20**	**21** Watch fireworks

1 When is Sarah going to have her birthday party? _____

_____

2 When are her parents going to celebrate their anniversary? _____

_____

3 When is her sister going to visit her friend? _____

_____

4 Is she going to watch the parade on the 17th? _____

5 Are they going to watch the fireworks on Saturday? _____

9 **Listen and match.**

JUNE						
SUNDAY	MONDAY	TUESDAY	WEDNESDAY	THURSDAY	FRIDAY	SATURDAY
					1	2
3	4	5	6	7	8	9
10	11	12	13	14	15	16
17	18	19	20	21	22	23
24	25	26	27	28	29	30

Mum's birthday

sports day

Father's Day

watch a parade

Grandparents' anniversary

Midsummer's Day

10 **Read and cross out the letters. Then write the special days.**

1 Cross out the first, third, fifth, ninth, tenth, twelfth and fourteenth letters.

G E T A B R T H L N D O A M Y

— — — — —   — — —

2 Cross out the first, third, seventh, tenth, thirteenth, sixteenth, seventeenth and twentieth letters.

B M O I D S R U M H M E P R S Y N D A O Y

— — — — — — — — — — ' — — — — —

3 Cross out the second, fourth, sixth, seventh, ninth, eleventh, sixteenth, seventeenth and nineteenth letters.

N A E H W P V Y I E N A R S D E V A E Y

— — — — — — — — — ' — — — — —

11 **Read and circle.**

Holi, The Festival of Colours

This festival takes place every spring to **watch** / **celebrate** the end of winter and the arrival of spring. It is celebrated in India, Nepal and other places. During Holi, people throw water and coloured **paper** / **powder**.

Tomatina, The Tomato Festival

Every year, on the last Wednesday of August, there is a **clean** / **messy** festival in Buñol, Spain, because people throw tomatoes at each other.

The Monkey Buffet

On the last weekend in November, the people of Lopburi, Thailand, invite hundreds of monkeys to a **feast** / **fight** of peanuts, fruit and vegetables.

Qoyllurit'i, The Festival of the Snow Star

It takes place every May or June on a **volcano** / **glacier** in Peru. People celebrate with music and dancing for three days and nights and the festival finishes with everyone leaving carrying torches.

12 **Circle T for true or F for false.**

1	The Festival of Colours takes place in China.	T	F
2	The Tomato Festival is celebrated in Spain.	T	F
3	The Monkey Buffet takes place at the end of November in Thailand.	T	F
4	People celebrate the Festival of the Snow Star for three weeks in Peru.	T	F

Think and write. What are you going to take with you?

THINK BIG

You're going to The Tomato Festival.

_____

You're going to the Festival of the Snow Star.

_____

13 **Read and answer the questions.**

> We usually say a year is 365 days long because that's about the time it takes for Earth to travel around the sun. It actually takes 365 days, 5 hours, 49 minutes and 12 seconds. The extra 5 hours, 49 minutes and 12 seconds add up to an extra day every four years on 29th February. This day is called *leap day*. Years with the extra day are called *leap years*. They can be divided evenly by four. For example, 2004, 2008 and 2012 were leap years.

1 How long does it take Earth to travel around the sun?

_____ days

_____ hours

_____ minutes

_____ seconds

2 How many days are there in a leap year? _____

14 **Solve these problems.**

1 Billy was born on 29th February, 2000. Write the next four years he can celebrate his birthday on 29th February.

_____   _____   _____   _____

2 It's 29th February, 2012. It's Jessi's birthday. Write the next four years she can celebrate her birthday on 29th February.

_____   _____   _____   _____

15 **Read and complete.**

> Greece   leap years   unlucky

   Julius Caesar created [1]_____ in the first century BC. Greeks and Romans were very superstitious about this year. They thought it was [2]_____ to start a journey, start a new job, marry or buy or sell something in a leap year. In [3]_____ some people still think it's very unlucky to marry on a leap day.

16 **Look and complete the email. Use the words in the box.**

FROM	¹_____
TO	alex@bigenglish.com
SUBJECT	²_____

³_____ Alex,

Guess what! It's our street carnival next weekend. There are loads of things planned. I'm going to watch the parade because my sister's in it. She's going to wear special traditional clothes. Then I'm going to buy a present for my grandparents. It's their anniversary on 13ᵗʰ June.

I've got to go. Write back soon!

⁴_____

Simon

Dear
Next weekend
simon@bigenglish.com
Your friend,

17 **Write an email to a friend. Invite your friend to a celebration.**

New Year's Day   Midsummer's Day party

FROM	
TO	
SUBJECT	

18 **Read and circle ue, e_e and ure.**

cute   glue   **bridge**
sponge   edge   picture
blue   cube
true   treasure

19 **Underline the words with ue, u_e and ure. Then read aloud.**

1 This is a huge bottle of glue.

2 I drink pure water.

20 **Connect the letters. Then write.**

1 bl	ure	**a** _ _ _ _ _ _
2 c	ue	**b** _ _ _ _
3 nat	ube	**c** _ _ _ _

3:19

21 **Listen and write.**

Hi, ¹ _____

Is it ² _____ ?

It's so ³ _____ ,

It's so ⁴ _____ ,

It's really ⁵ _____ !

Is that a monster

In the ⁶ _____ ?

22 **Read and answer.**

Sam's going to the dentist on the ninth of March. On the fifteenth of March, he's going to visit his aunt and uncle. His cousins are on holiday so on the twentieth of March, he is going to visit them. They're going to go to the cinema together.

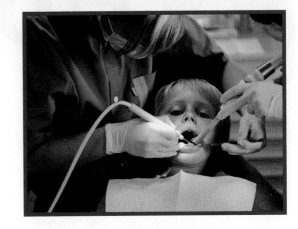

1 Where is Sam going on 9th March? _____

2 What is he going to do on 15th March? _____

3 Is he going to see his cousins on 15th? _____

4 Is he going to see his cousins on 20th? _____

23 **Read and match.**

1 give a		**a**	clothes
2 have a		**b**	a present
3 watch a		**c**	parade
4 watch		**d**	party
5 wear different		**e**	card
6 get		**f**	fireworks

24 **Read and write. Use the words in the box.**

During   For   last   takes place

1 The Festival of Colours _____ every year in India.

2 _____ three days and nights people celebrate with music.

3 The Tomato Festival is on the _____ Wednesday in August.

4 _____ the Monkey Buffet Festival, monkeys feast on fruit and vegetables.

unit 8 Hobbies

1 **Draw the path. Connect the pictures. Then complete the question and answer.**

football player → painter → toy car collection → chess player →

coin collection → singer → video game player → shell collection →

doll collection → dancer → basketball player → writer

What _____?

_____

2 Listen and circle. Then answer the questions.

The Best and the Worst

Matthew collects toy cars.
He's got one hundred and seven.
But Pam's **car / shell** collection is bigger
She's got three hundred and
Eleven / ten!

Kay is good at games
She's really good at **music / chess**.
But Paul is even better than Kay.
And Liz, well, she's the best!

What's your hobby, Bobby?
What do you like doing?
What's your hobby, Bobby?
What is fun for you?

Steve is a **great / terrible** singer.
Emma's worse than Steve.
But David's singing is the worst.
When he sings, people leave!

It's **bad / good** to have a hobby.
Some people have got a few.
Even if you're not the best,
It still is fun to do!

Chorus

1 Who collects toy cars? _____

2 How many cars has Matthew got? _____

3 How many cars has Pam got? _____

4 Who is the best at games? _____

5 Is Steve a good singer? _____

6 Do people like listening to David's singing? _____

3 Read. Then circle **T** for true or **F** for false.

The School Play

Christina's dad is excited about this year's school play. The play is *Snow White*. He wants Christina to be a star in the play. He wants her to be an important character, like Snow White or the Evil Queen. Christina hasn't got those parts. Her friends Lizzie and Ruth have got those parts because they're better singers and actors than Christina. But Christina's the tallest girl in the class, so she's going to be a tree. It's a small part but Christina's dad is very proud of her.

1	Christina's dad thinks the school play is boring.	T	F
2	He wants Christina to be Snow White.	T	F
3	Christina is a better singer than Lizzie.	T	F
4	Christina is taller than all the other girls.	T	F
5	Christina's going to be a tree.	T	F

4 Write about you.

1 What character would you like to be in *Snow White*? Why?

_____

2 What are you good at?

_____

 THINK BIG Think about Snow White and the Evil Queen. Who do you like better? Why? Use the words in the box.

friendly
kind   nice
old   pretty

_____

5 Listen and stick. Then number and write. Use the words in the box.

> the best   the coolest   the worst

a
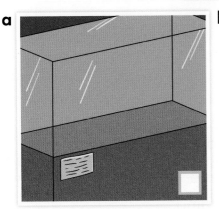

_____

b
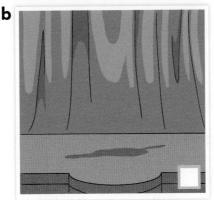

_____

c

_____

6 Complete the table. Use the words in the box.

> bad   the best   better   the worst

	worse		good		

7 Read and circle the correct words. Then match.

1 Susan's team is **good** / **better** at basketball. ☐

2 Cassie's story is the **longer** / **longest** story. ☐

3 Grandpa used to be the **good** / **best** painter in the city. ☐

4 Diane is worse **than** / **of** Claire at video games. ☐

5 Jason has a **better** / **good** shell collection than Craig. ☐

6 This is the **oldest** / **older** doll in my collection. ☐

a

b

c

d

e

f

8 **Read. Then use a form of big or old to complete each sentence.**

> Philip's got two brothers and three sisters. Pablo's got three brothers and four sisters. Tony's got two brothers and two sisters.

1 Philip's family is _____ Tony's.

2 Pablo's family is _____ of all.

3 Tony's family is _____.

> Dean's grandma is eighty-six years old. Betty's grandma is seventy-four years old. Harriet's grandma is ninety-one years old.

4 Dean's grandma is _____ Betty's grandma.

5 Betty's grandma is _____.

6 Harriet's grandma is _____ of all.

9 **Read and answer for you.**

1 What are you good at?

_____

2 What is your mum or dad good at?

_____

3 What is your brother or sister good at?

_____

4 What are you bad at?

_____

5 What is your best friend bad at?

_____

6 What is your cousin bad at?

_____

10 **Number the photos.**

1 butterfly collection   **2** doll's house   **3** embroidery   **4** football

a    b    c    d

11 **Read and circle the four mistakes. Then write the correct words.**

drawing   employers   rocking   thread

1 Many football clubs in the 19th century were started by teachers so that the workers could play and stay fit.   _____

2 Many girls liked doing embroidery with a needle and rope. They used to embroider cushions and tablecloths.   _____

3 Girls in the 19th century used to play with dolls and jumping horses. Boys used to play with toy trains and railways.   _____

4 People in the 19th century loved nature. One popular hobby was collecting and playing with butterflies.   _____

Think and write.

THINK BIG

collecting butterflies   dolls   embroidery   football
marbles   rocking horse   tennis   trains   TV   video games

19th century   21st century

Read and match. Write the numbers.

a  b  c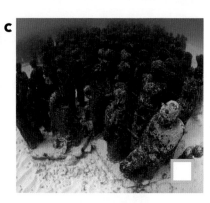

1 This is a museum that has 400 sculptures. If you want to visit this place you have to swim there. Don't forget your swimming trunks or swimming costume.

2 This museum holds a festival every year. Many experts come to speak at the festival.

3 This is a museum that has pieces of hair. Each one has a person's name and the date it was cut. The hair is displayed in a cave in Turkey.

13 **Think of your own weird collection in a museum. Draw and then describe it.**

14 **Look and complete the informal letter. Use the words in the box.**

Beach View Hotel,
10 Pebble lane,
Dorset,
DT1 XF2

12th August, 2014
Dear
How are you?
Love,

1 _____

2 _____ Mia,

3 _____ I'm fine.

We're staying at the Beach View Hotel in Dorset and it's great! I'm starting a shell collection. I got lots yesterday. I went to the beach and saw them on the sand. The best one is beautiful and pink. I think it's my best shell yet. I'm having a great time on holiday. It's hot and sunny. Tomorrow we're going on a hike and maybe to the cinema in the evening.

When I get home, I'll bring my photos and shells round to show you.

4 _____

Beth

15 **Write an informal letter to a friend. Tell your friend about a hobby. Here are some ideas:**

a healthy hobby   a creative hobby   a hobby that helps you learn

_____

_____

_____

_____

_____

_____

_____

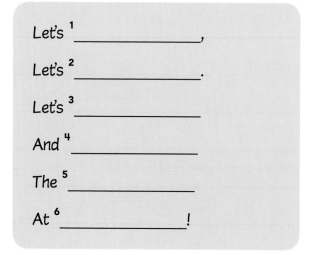
Phonics | *y, igh*

16 **Read and circle y and igh.**

fly   try   light

high   my   picture

cute

true

sky   fight   night

17 **Underline the words with y and igh. Then read aloud.**

1 Birds fly high in the sky.

2 I watch the moon at night.

18 **Connect the letters. Then write.**

1 li   y   **a** _ _ _

2 m   ght   **b** _ _ _ _ _

3 fl   y   **c** _ _

3:36
19 **Listen and write.**

Let's **1** _____,

Let's **2** _____.

Let's **3** _____

And **4** _____

The **5** _____

At **6** _____!

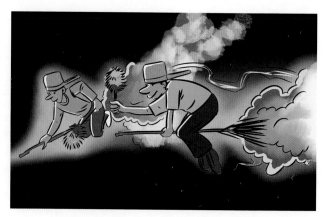

20 **Complete the dialogues with forms of bad, good and old.**

1

A: Carol is _____ at chess.

B: Yes. But Henry is _____ Carol.

A: That's true. But I'm _____ of all.

2

A: Sean is a _____ singer.

B: I know! But Chris is _____ Sean.

A: Yes. But Brian is _____ singer of all.

3

A: Patty's grandma is 80. That's _____.

B: Yes. But Marge's grandma is _____ her. She's 85.

A: I know. And Randy's grandma is _____ of all. She's 95.

21 **Answer about your family. Write complete sentences.**

1 Who is the best singer? _____

2 Who is the worst singer? _____

3 Who is the best dancer? _____

4 Who is the worst dancer? _____

5 Who is the oldest person? _____

22 **Read and circle.**

1 In 19th century, dolls **was / were** made of china.

2 Football was **give / given** rules for the first time.

3 Girls **use to / used to** embroider cushions.

4 Collecting butterflies **was / were** a popular hobby.

Learning New Things

1 Solve the puzzle. Write the words in the boxes.

Across →

1

_____ like a rock star

2

draw _____ books

3

_____

4

make a _____

Down ↓

5

_____ a cake

6

build a _____

7

play the _____

8

_____ like a
hip-hop artist

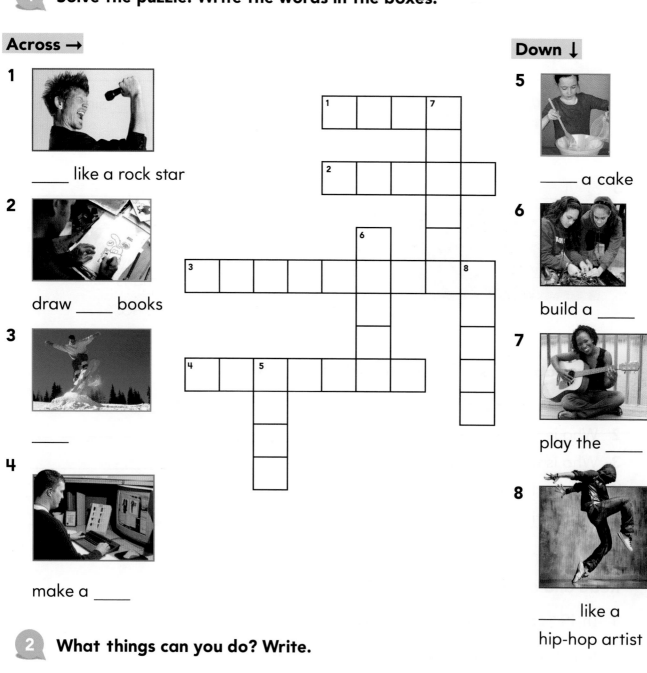

2 What things can you do? Write.

_____

_____

3 **Listen and write. Use the words in the box.**

> bake   draw   learn   show   sing
> skateboard   speak

Learning Is Fun!

Do you know how to ¹_____?
It's so brilliant. It's so cool!
I can ²_____ you how to do it
On Friday after school.

It's fun to learn new things,
Like how to ³_____
Or ⁴_____ or ⁵_____
!
I wish I had a lot more free time.
I would try to ⁶_____ everything!

I'd like to learn to speak English.
"It's hard!" my friends all say.
But I think it's really interesting.
I'd like to ⁷_____ it well one day.

Chorus

> Do you want
> to learn English?

> Yes!

4 **What activities are amazing, dangerous and difficult? Write.**

1 I think it's amazing to _____

_____.

2 I think it's dangerous to _____

_____.

3 I think it's difficult to _____

_____.

Story

5 **Read. Then circle.**

The Best in the Class

Christina and Sam are walking home from school. They see Jake, a boy from Sam's class, in the park. He's really good at playing the guitar. Sam can't play the guitar but he'd like to learn. Jake tries to teach Sam to play the guitar. Sam isn't very good. Christina thinks Sam is terrible at playing the guitar.

1 Jake is in Sam's **class / football team**.

2 He is good at playing the **piano / guitar**.

3 Sam **can / can't** play the guitar.

4 He **would / wouldn't** like to learn how to play the guitar.

5 Sam **is / isn't** very good at playing the guitar.

6 **Write about you.**

I'd like to learn how to _____.

I'm good at _____.

I'm not very good at _____.

THINK BIG

What happens next in the story? Use these ideas or think of your own.

1 Sam practises every day and learns how to play the guitar very well.

2 Sam goes home and plays video games.

3 Jake teaches Sam to play the guitar very well.

3:45

7 **Listen and stick. Then write.**

learn to dance   learn to draw   learn to play tennis   learn to skateboard

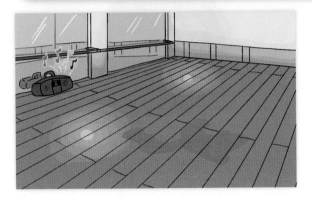

1 _____

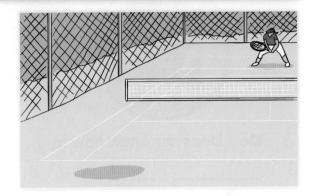

2 _____

3 _____

4 _____

8 **Look at 7. Complete the questions and write answers.**

1 What would he _____

_____?

_____

2 What would she _____

_____?

_____

3 What would she _____

_____?

_____

4 What would she _____

_____?

_____

9 **Look. Then circle and complete.**

1

Do / **Does** she know how to

_____?

_____. Her cakes
taste delicious.

2

Do / **Does** you know how to

_____?

_____. But I can
play tennis.

3

Do **he** / **they** know how to

_____?

_____. They are
building one right now.

4

你好

Does **we** / **she** know how to

_____?

_____. But she
speaks English very well.

10 **Write the questions and answers.**

1 What does he think of snowboarding? _____ (*fun*)

2 What do you think of making websites? _____ (*boring*)

3 _____ They think it's difficult.
(*dancing*)

4 _____ She thinks it's amazing.
(*drawing comic books*)

11 **Number the sentences in order.**

_____ Her muscles contract and she hits the ball.

_____ The tennis player wants to hit the ball.

_____ Her nerves send a message to her muscles.

_____ Her brain tells her nerves that she wants to hit the ball.

12 **Choose the correct answers.**

1 Your muscles, joints and _____ make up your musculoskeletal system.

    a bones   **b** nerves   **c** organs

2 _____ make your body move by pulling your bones in different directions.

    a Organs   **b** Nerves   **c** Muscles

3 Muscles move by _____ and relaxing.

    a building   **b** contracting   **c** sending a message

4 Your _____ send messages to your muscles.

    a joints   **b** nerves   **c** organs

5 _____ connect two or more bones to each other.

    a Joints   **b** Muscles   **c** Nerves

6 Your _____ are your body's frame.

    a muscles   **b** joints   **c** bones

Think about your body. Complete the sentences.

THINK BIG

1 Without _____

_____ .

2 It's amazing that _____

_____ .

13 **Read about Yuto Miyazawa. Then imagine what he would say and write.**

Yuto Miyazawa was a professional musician when he was only eight years old!

He was on TV and performed at Madison Square Garden. He even played with famous musicians like Ozzy Osbourne, Les Paul and G.E. Smith.

1 Would you like to learn how to play another instrument?

Yuto: _____

2 Do you always like playing the guitar?

Yuto: _____

3 What do you think of playing with famous musicians?

Yuto: _____

14 **Now write about you. Explain your answers.**

1 Would you like to learn how to play the guitar?

_____

_____

2 By sixteen, Gregory Smith had several college degrees and travelled the world helping young people. Would you like to be like him?

_____

_____

3 What do you think of these extraordinary kids?

_____

_____

15 **Look and complete the review. Use the words in the box.**

acting
builds
Film
filmgirl123
funny
night
recommend
yourself

Reviewed by ¹_____

★ ★ ★ ★

A Great ²_____ for Everyone!

Kara Makes a Robot is a ³_____ film. I watched it last ⁴_____ and I really liked it. It is not a long film. It's only about eighty minutes but there is a lot of great ⁵_____ in it.

It's about a girl named Kara. She ⁶_____ a robot. At first, they are friends but soon the robot starts doing silly things. It's very funny and exciting. I don't want to tell you too much. You should watch it for ⁷_____.

Kara Makes a Robot is a great film and I ⁸_____ it to everyone!

16 **Write a review of a film, book or TV show you like.**

Reviewed by _____

_____

_____

_____

_____

_____

_____

_____

_____

_____

17 **Read and circle ew, ey and e_e.**

new   grey   hey

stew   bake

those   eve

stay

few   they   these

18 **Underline the words with ew, ey and e_e. Then read aloud.**

1 I've got a few of these grey scarves.

2 Hey, they've got a new board game.

19 **Connect the letters. Then write.**

1	th	ew	**a** _ _ _
2	f	ese	**b** _ _ _ _ _
3	n	ey	**c** _ _ _ _
4	pr	ew	**d** _ _ _

3:53

20 **Listen and write.**

¹ _____ three are

² _____ !

They eat ³ _____

And wear ⁴ _____, too!

21 **Read and match.**

1 Without working joints,

2 By pulling your bones,

3 Your nerves send

a a message to your muscles.

b your body wouldn't be able to move.

c your muscles help your body move.

22 **Look at the chart. Write questions and answers.**

What do they think of...?			
Luisa	interesting	amazing	boring
Martin	interesting	cool	fun

1 What does Luisa think of drawing comic books?

_____

2 _____

They think it's interesting.

3 What does Martin think of singing like a rock star?

_____

23 **Answer the questions in complete sentences.**

1 Does Phil know how to speak Chinese? (*no/but/speak Spanish*)

_____

2 What would they like to learn how to do? (*build a robot*)

_____

3 What does she want to learn how to do? (*dance like a hip-hop artist*)

_____

1 **Make guesses about Ben and ✓ the answers.**

Look at the happy and sad faces on Ben's calendar. Ben thinks some days are the best. He thinks some days are the worst.

1 What is Ben like?

- ☐ friendly
- ☐ good at chess
- ☐ serious
- ☐ funny
- ☐ good at sports
- ☐ clever

2 What would Ben like to do?

- ☐ have a party
- ☐ learn to play chess
- ☐ watch fireworks
- ☐ learn to snowboard
- ☐ play video games
- ☐ watch TV

Sun	Mon
31st Dec. NEW YEAR'S EVE	**1**st Jan. ?
☺ ☺ ☺	
7th LEARN HOW TO	**8**th MEET FRIENDS
☹ ☹ ☹	SHARE COLLECTION ☺ ☺

2 **Write on Ben's calendar. Write a hobby or things for Ben to learn on the tenth and the thirteenth.**

Make a guess about these two days.

3 **Look at the calendar. Make guesses and write the answers.**

1 What's Ben going to do on Monday?

_____

2 What special day is on Saturday the sixth?

_____

BEN'S CALENDAR

Tues	Wed	Thurs	Fri	Sat
2nd MEET FRIENDS SHARE COLLECTION ☺ ☺	**3rd** PRACTISE THE PIANO ☹ ☹	**4th** LEARN TO PLAY ☺ ☺ ☺	**5th** BAKE MUM'S BIRTHDAY CAKE ☺ ☺ ☺	**6th** ?
9th PRACTISE FOOTBALL ☹ ☹ ☹ *The best!*	**10th** ? ___ ☺ ☺ ☺	**11th** MAKE A WEBSITE ☺ ☺ ☺	**12th** LEARN TO PLAY BADMINTON ☹ ☹ *The worst!*	**13th** ? ___ ☹ ☹ ☹

4 **What do you think of Ben? Would you like to be Ben's friend? Write a letter about Ben to your parents. Begin:**

Dear Mum and Dad,

I've got a new classmate. His name is Ben. _____

_____

_____

_____

_____

_____

_____

_____

| Who is **taller**, Chris or Tom? | Chris is **taller than** Tom. |

old	→	old**er**
big	→	big**ger**
heavy	→	heav**ier**

1 **Read. Write the answers.**

1 What is bigger? An elephant or a cat?

An elephant is _____ a cat.

2 What is heavier? A notebook or a computer?

A computer is _____ a notebook.

3 Who is older? Your grandmother or your aunt?

_____

4 Who is taller? Your brother/sister or your father?

_____

5 What is smaller? A baseball or a basketball?

_____

| My sister's hair is longer than **my hair**. | My sister's hair is longer than **mine**. |
| My sister's hair is longer than **your hair**. | My sister's hair is longer than **yours**. |

2 **Circle the correct words.**

1 **Your / Yours** backpack is heavy. But my backpack is heavier than **your / yours**.

2 **Their / Theirs** hair is long. But my hair is longer than **their / theirs**.

3 **Her / Hers** brother is younger than **my / mine**.

4 **Our / Ours** classroom is bigger than **their / theirs** classroom.

5 **My / Mine** friend is taller than Shaun's.

6 **He / His** shoes are smaller than **her / hers** shoes.

| **Where** is | he/she | going after school? | He/She | is going to football practice. |
| **What** are | you | doing tonight? | We | are watching a DVD at home. |

1 **Look. Write What or Where. Answer the questions.**

walk the dog

visit the dentist

1 _____ is she doing after school today?

She _____.

2 _____ are they going on Saturday?

They _____.

play video games

go to the shopping centre

3 _____ is he doing tonight?

He _____.

4 _____ are you going tonight?

We _____.

| **How often** does | he/she | have a guitar lesson? | **How often** do | you/they | go to school? |

2 **Circle the correct questions. Write the answers.**

1 **How often do / How often does** they do the dishes?

| Mon | Tues |

_____ a week.

2 **How often do / How often does** she visit her cousins?

| Sun |

_____ a week.

| What **would** you **like**? | | | **I'd like** some soup. | | I'd like → I would like |
| What would | he/she | **like**? | He'**d**/She'**d** | **like** yoghurt. | He'd/She'd like → He/She would like |

1 **Look. Write questions. Write the answers.**

1 What would she like for breakfast?

_____ eggs on toast.

2 What _____ for a snack?

_____

3 _____

_____ for dessert?

_____

Favourite Food Survey

1 Stacy: eggs on toast for breakfast

2 Martin: steamed buns for a snack

3 Stacy and Martin: yoghurt and watermelon for dessert

| **Would** | you
he/she
they | **like to try** some curry? | **Yes,** | I
we
he/she
they | **would.** | **No,** | I
we
he/she
they | **wouldn't.** |

2 **Complete the dialogue. Use the correct form of do, would or like.**

1 **A:** Does Paula like Mexican food?

B: Yes, _____.

A: _____ she _____ to try some chili?

B: Yes, she would. She loves chilli.

2 **A:** Do you like hot drinks?

B: No, _____.

A: Would you like to try some lemonade?

B: No, _____. Thanks anyway.

I		I	
You		You	
He/She	**should** eat healthy food.	He/She	**shouldn't** stay up late.
We		We	
They		They	

1 **Write sentences with should and shouldn't. Use the ideas in the boxes.**

1 I've got a fever.

_____

_____

> go to school today
>
> rest

2 Her tooth hurts.

_____

_____

> go to the dentist
>
> eat so many sweets

3 Ted fell and hurt his knee.

_____

_____

> go to basketball practice
>
> see the school nurse

4 Some children always feel tired.

_____

_____

> watch so much TV
>
> get more exercise

I		**myself.**
You		**yourself.**
He/She	should take care of	**himself/herself.**
We		**ourselves.**
They		**themselves.**

2 **Look at 1. Complete the sentences. Use herself, himself, themselves or yourself.**

1 You should take care of _____.

2 She should take care of _____.

3 He _____.

4 They _____.

Unit 5 | Extra Grammar Practice

How many chimpanzees were there 100 years ago?	There **were** more than one million. But now there **are** only about 200,000.

1 **Complete the sentences.**

Animal	Habitat	Population in the Past	Population Now
 Mexican walking fish	streams and rivers in Mexico	a lot	almost none

¹_____ Mexican walking fish ² _____ in Mexico now?

³_____ a lot of Mexican walking fish in Mexican streams and rivers in the past?

Now, ⁴_____ almost none. In the past, ⁵_____ a lot.

Why are chimpanzees endangered?	They're endangered **because** people are moving into their habitat.

2 **Answer the questions. Use the information in the box and because.**

> their habitat's polluted
>
> people are keeping them as pets

1 Why is the Egyptian tortoise endangered?

It is endangered _____

_____.

2 Why are Andean flamingos endangered?

_____

_____.

Did people **have** cars in 1950?	Yes, they **did**.
Did people **have** cars in 1900?	No, they **didn't**. They travelled by horse and carriage or by train.
Before TV, what **did** people **use to do** for entertainment at night?	They **used to listen** to the radio.

 1 **Read. Then answer the questions. Use did or didn't, do or don't, use or used.**

Then and Now

1930's – People usually listened to the radio. They didn't own TVs.

Today – People sometimes listen to the radio. Most people watch TV.

1950's – People wrote letters by hand.

Today – Many people write letters on the computer.

1970's – Young people played outdoor games, like hide and seek.

Today – Many people, young and old, play video games.

1 Did people listen to the radio years ago?

Yes, _____ because they didn't have TVs.

Do people listen to the radio now?

Yes, _____ but they usually watch TV.

2 Did people use to write letters on the computer a long time ago?

_____

Do they write letters on the computer now?

_____

3 Before video games, what _____ young people

_____ to do for fun?

They _____ to play hide and seek outdoors.

When **are**	you	**going to have** the party?	I	**am going to have** it on Monday.
	they		We	**are going to have** it on Monday.
When **is**	he/she	**going to visit** Grandma?	They	
			He/She	**is going to visit** her next month.
Are you/they going to visit Grandma **on the ninth**?			Yes, **on the ninth**.	
Is he/she going to visit Grandma **on the fifth**?			No, **on the ninth**.	

1 **Complete the questions and answers. Use going to and the words in the box.**

fourth   second   third   twenty-second

1

give a present 2ⁿᵈ July

When _____ your dad

_____ to your mum?

On the _____.

2

watch a parade 22ⁿᵈ April

When _____ they

_____ a parade?

_____

3

wear different clothes 4ᵗʰ July

When _____ you

_____ different clothes?

_____

4

have a party 3ʳᵈ July

When _____ you

_____ a party?

_____

2 **Look and write.**

1 fourteenth _____   **2** eighth _____   **3** thirtieth _____   **4** first _____

Katie is a **good** chess player.	My brother's paintings are **bad**.
Katie is a **better** chess player **than** Jeff.	My sister's paintings are **worse than** his.
Katie is **the best** chess player in the class.	My paintings are **the worst** of all.

1 **Look and complete the sentences.**

1 (big)

	Number of shells
John	85
Mike	250
Sally	1000

John loves collecting shells. His collection is ¹_____. Mike's collection is ²_____ John's. But Sally has got ³_____ in the whole class. She started when she was six.

2 (good)

	Wins
Ella	10
Stephanie	4
Tania	6

Ella is good at video games. She is ¹_____ in the class. Stephanie is a ²_____ video game player. But Tania practises a lot. She's ³_____ Stephanie.

3 (bad)

	Losses
The Bears	5
The Tigers	3
The Lions	4

The Bears, Tigers and Lions are popular baseball teams but they are not having a good year. The Bears team is ¹_____ of the three teams this year. The Lions are ²_____ than the Tigers. But the Tigers are pretty ³_____, too.

2 **Look and match.**

1 He's good   **a** good at climbing trees.

2 She's not very   **b** are bad at football.

3 They   **c** at music.

Do you **know how to play** the piano?			Yes, I do. / No, I don't.	
What would	you	like to learn how to do?	I'd	like to **learn how to play** the piano.
	he/she		He'd/She'd	
	they		They'd	

1 Read. Then answer the questions. Use the words in the box.

> bake a cake   make a website   sing like a rock star

1 Jeff and Tina are going to have singing lessons next year. What would they like to learn?

_____

2 Sue loves cakes. She's having a baking class now. What would she like to learn?

_____

3 Bryan loves computers. He is having a web-design class now. What would he like to learn?

_____

What do you **think of** ballet?	I think it's boring.
What does he **think of** hip-hop music?	He thinks it's cool.

2 Complete the dialogues.

1 A: What do _____

_____ ?

B: I _____ it's cool.

2 A: What does _____

_____ ?

B: She _____ it's a lot of fun.

Young Learners English Practice: Listening A

– 5 questions –

Listen and look. There is one example.

Getting Ready for School

Time Susan woke up: _____7:30_____

1 What she's having for breakfast: _____

2 How she's getting to school: _____

3 What homework she did for today: _____

4 What she's doing after school: _____

5 Her chore for today: _____

Young Learners English Practice: Listening B

– 5 questions –

3:58

Listen and look. There is one example.

What is Martin's hobby?

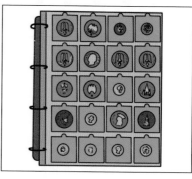

A ☐   **B** ☐   **C** ☑

1   What does Jane like doing?

A ☐   **B** ☐   **C** ☐

2   Which instrument does Anthony know how to play?

A ☐   **B** ☐   **C** ☐

3 What is the boy's favourite sport?

A ☐

B ☐

C ☐

4 What is the class going to do?

A ☐

B ☐

C ☐

5 What are they going to do later on?

A ☐

B ☐

C ☐

Young Learners English Practice: Reading & Writing A

– 6 questions –

Look and read. Write yes or no.

Examples

The dog knows how to ride a skateboard. _____ *yes* _____

The little boy knows how to ride a bicycle. _____ *no* _____

Questions

1 The girls know how to play tennis.

   _____

2 The man can sing well.

   _____

3 The bird knows how to talk.

   _____

4 The woman is going to cross the street.

   _____

5 A parade is coming.

   _____

6 You can see fireworks in the sky.

   _____

Young Learners English Practice: Reading & Writing B

– 6 questions –

Look and read. Choose the correct words and write them on the lines.

a slide

chess

a guitar

a birthday cake

actors

a comic book

a video game

a robot

Example

This is a game you play on a computer or TV screen.

<u>a video game</u>

Questions

1 This is a musical instrument with strings.

_____

2 These are the people in a play or film.

_____

3 This is a game you play on a board by moving pieces.

_____

4 This is a book that tells a story with pictures and speech bubbles.

_____

5 This is a machine which does work for people.

_____

6 This is something people often eat on their birthdays.

_____

Young Learners English Practice: Reading & Writing C

– 5 questions –

Read the text and choose the best answer.

Paul is talking to his friend Vicky.

Example

Vicky: Hi, Paul. What are you doing?

Paul: A I'm fine, thank you.

B I had a party.

C I'm making a cake.

Questions

1 **Vicky:** What is it for?

Paul: A It's for my parents' anniversary.

B On the last day of the year.

C It's two days until Mother's Day.

Young Learners English Practice: Reading & Writing C

2 Vicky: Would you like some help?

   Paul: A   OK. What time?

                B   Sure, I would love to.

                C   That would be great.

3 Vicky: What would you like me to do?

   Paul: A   You can beat the eggs.

                B   No thanks, I don't like eggs.

                C   Two eggs are better than one.

4 Vicky: Should I use this bowl?

   Paul: A   It's not as big as the other one.

                B   No, use the bigger one.

                C   Because I like it.

5 Vicky: And then what are we going to do?

   Paul: A   Mix everything and put it in the oven.

                B   Flour, eggs and milk.

                C   The oven is hot now.

6 Vicky: When will it be finished?

   Paul: A   Every once in a while.

                B   In about an hour.

                C   It lasts a long time.

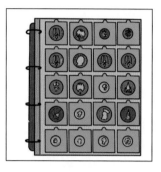

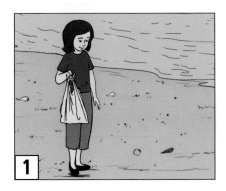

Extra Verb Practice

Base Form	Simple Past		Base Form	Simple Past
ask	_____		fly	_____
_____	baked		_____	got
be	_____		give	_____
_____	began		_____	went
bring	_____		grow	_____
_____	built		_____	had
buy	_____		hear	_____
_____	called		_____	helped
catch	_____		hit	_____
_____	celebrated		_____	held
change	_____		hope	_____
_____	came		_____	kept
cook	_____		kill	_____
_____	cut		_____	knew
destroy	_____		learn	_____
_____	did		_____	left
draw	_____		like	_____
_____	drank		_____	listened
drive	_____		live	_____
_____	ate		_____	looked
explain	_____		lose	_____
_____	fell		_____	loved
feed	_____		make	_____
_____	felt		_____	met
fight	_____		move	_____
_____	found		_____	needed

Base Form	Simple Past	Base Form	Simple Past
perform	_____	tell	_____
_____	planned	_____	thought
play	_____	throw	_____
_____	put	_____	travelled
read	_____	try	_____
_____	realised	_____	turned
rest	_____	understand	_____
_____	rode	_____	used
ring	_____	visit	_____
_____	ran	_____	waited
say	_____	wake up	_____
_____	saw	_____	walked
sell	_____	want	_____
_____	sent	_____	washed
sing	_____	watch	_____
_____	sat	_____	wore
skateboard	_____	worry	_____
_____	slept	_____	wrote
snowboard	_____	yell	_____
_____	spoke		
stand	_____		
_____	started		
stay up	_____		
_____	swam		
take	_____		
_____	talked		

My Pen Pal

I'd like to tell you about my

pen pal. _____ name is
 (His/Her)

_____ .
 (Name)

_____ lives in
 (He/She)

_____ .
 (City, Country)

1

He/She likes _____
 (activity)

and _____ .
 (activity)

_____ wants to visit me here
 (He/She)

in _____ , too!
 (where I live)

4

_____ loves eating
(Name)

_____ food.
(adjective)

favourite dish is _____
(His/Her)   (food)

(He/She) _____ eats it _____
                            (how often)

I'd like to try it, too!

2

_____ has got
(Name)

_____ hair.
(adjective)   (His/Her)

hair is _____
(adjective)

(He/She) _____ is really
                      (adjective)

_____
(adjective)

3

sore eyes

ate too many sweets

have a cold

sore throat

have a cough

used the computer too much

stomachache

played too many video games

allergies while playing outside

sneezing

drank too much lemonade

watched too much TV

SCHOOL TALENT SHOW

Wednesday, 9th May

6:00 P.M.–7:30 P.M.

School Auditorium

Vote for the best talent!

Sign up to perform by Friday, 4th May.

My BIG ENGLISH World

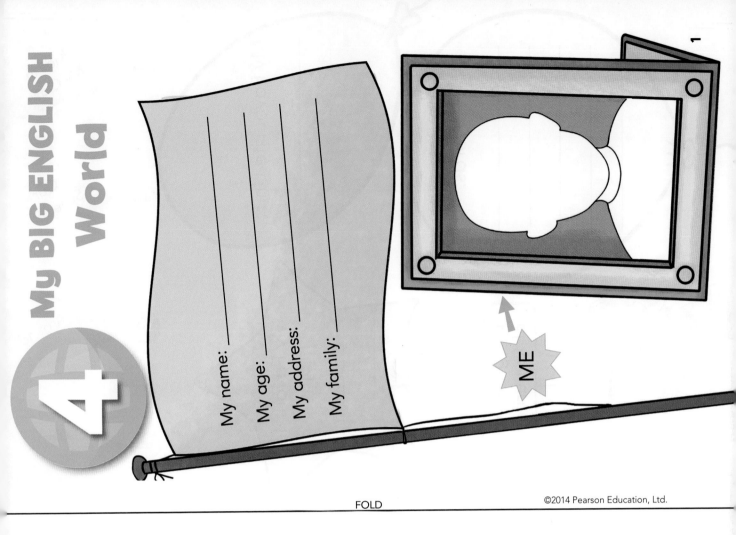

My name: _____

My age: _____

My address: _____

My family: _____

ME

FOLD

ENGLISH

AROUND ME

Look around you. Paste or draw things with English words. Write everyday words and sentences.

Everyday Words

Everyday Sentences

Henry's Chocolate

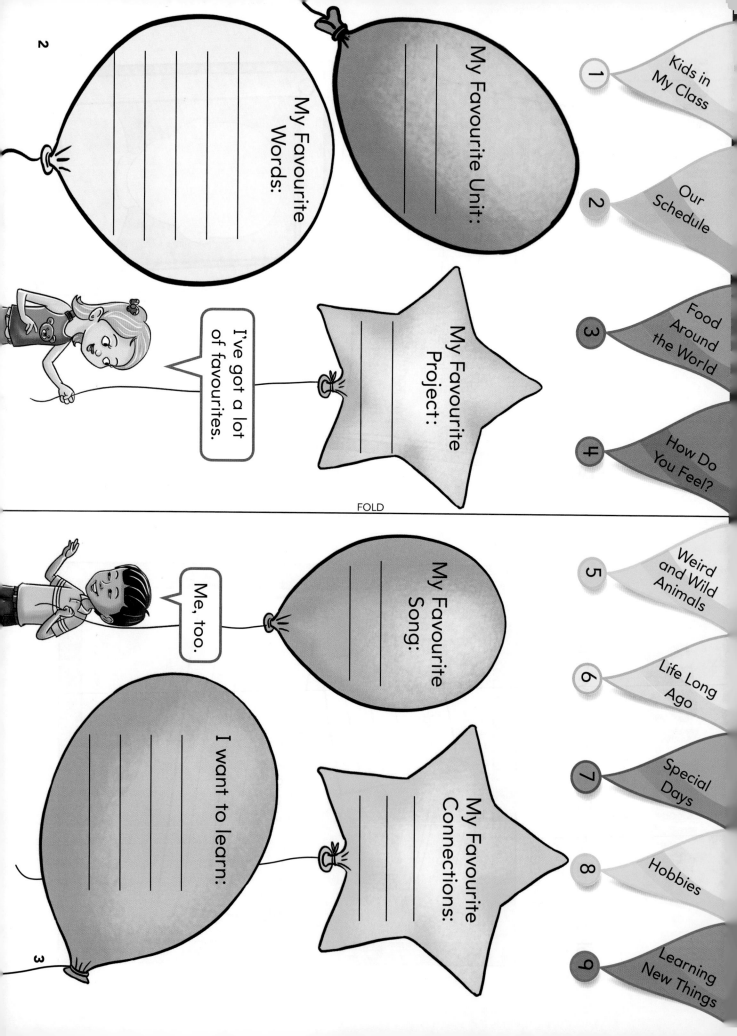

Unit 1, page 5

Unit 2, page 15

Unit 3, page 25

Unit 4, page 37

Unit 5, page 47

Unit 6, page 57

Unit 7, page 69

Unit 8, page 79

Unit 9, page 89